THE NATIONAL
NURSERY BOOK

[ZHINGOORA BOOKS]

CONTENTS.

PREFACE.

The Publishers offer in this little volume well known and long loved stories to their young readers. The tales which have delighted the children of many generations will, they feel assured, be equally welcome in the nurseries of the present day, which, with the popularity and antiquity of the contents of the volume, justify them in styling it The National Nursery Book.

RED RIDING-HOOD.

Once upon a time there lived on the borders of a great forest a woodman and his wife who had one little daughter, a sweet, kind child, whom every one loved. She was the joy of her mother's heart, and to please her, the good woman made her a little scarlet cloak and hood, and the child looked so pretty in it that everybody called her Little Red Riding-Hood.

RED RIDING HOOD PREPARING FOR HER JOURNEY.

One day her mother told her she meant to send her to her grandmother—a very old woman who lived in the heart of the wood—to take her some fresh butter and new-laid eggs and a nice cake. Little Red Riding-Hood was very pleased to be sent on this errand, for she liked to do kind things, and it was so very long since she had seen her grandmother that she had almost forgotten what the dame looked like.

LITTLE RED RIDING HOOD GATHERING FLOWERS.

THE WOLF.

The sun was shining brightly, but it was not too warm under the shade of the old trees, and Red Riding-Hood sang with glee as she gathered a great bunch of wild flowers to give to her grandmother. She sang so sweetly that a cushat dove flew down from a tree and followed her. Now, it happened that a wolf, a very cruel, greedy creature, heard her song also, and longed to eat her for his breakfast, but he knew Hugh, the woodman, was at work very near, with his great dog, and he feared they might hear Red Riding-Hood cry out, if he frightened her, and then they would kill him. So he came up to her very gently and said, "Good day, Little Red Riding-Hood; where are you going?"

"To see my grandmother," said the child, "and take her a present from mother of eggs and butter and cake."

"Where does your grandmamma live?" asked the wolf.

"Quite in the middle of the wood," she replied.

"Oh! I think I know the house. Good day, Red Riding-Hood." And the wolf ran off as fast as he could

AT PLAY IN THE WOOD.

Little Red Riding-Hood was not in a hurry, and there were many things to amuse her in the wood. She ran after the white and yellow butterflies that danced before her, and sometimes she caught one, but she always let it go again, for she never liked to hurt any creature.

THE WOLF FOLLOWS LITTLE RED RIDING HOOD.

And then there were the merry, cunning little squirrels to watch, cracking nuts on the branches of the old trees, and every now and then a rabbit would hurry away through the tall ferns, or a great bee come buzzing near her, and she would stop to watch it gathering honey from the flowers, and wild thyme. So she went on very slowly. By-and-by she saw Hugh, the woodman. "Where are you going, Little Red Riding-Hood," said he, "all alone?"

LITTLE RED RIDING HOOD CATCHING BUTTERFLIES.

"I am going to my grandmamma's," said the child. "Good day; I must make haste now, for it grows late."

GRANDMOTHER AND THE WOLF.

While Little Red Riding-Hood was at play in the wood, the great wolf galloped on as fast as he could to the old woman's house. Grandmother lived all by herself, but once or twice a-day a neighbour's child came to tidy her house and get her food. Now, grandmother was very feeble, and often kept her bed; and it happened that she was in bed the day Little Red Riding-Hood went to see her. When the wolf reached the cottage door he tapped.

"Who is there?" asked the old dame.

"Little Red Riding-Hood, granny," said the wolf, trying to speak like the child.

"Come in, my dear," said the old lady, who was a little deaf. "Pull the string and the latch will come up."

The wolf did as she told him, went in, and you may think how frightened poor grandmother was when she saw him standing by her bed instead of Little Red Riding-Hood.

RED RIDING-HOOD AT THE DOOR.

Very soon the wolf, who was quite hungry after his run, eat up poor grandmother. Indeed, she was not enough for his breakfast, and so he thought he would like to eat sweet Red Riding-Hood also. Therefore he dressed himself in granny's nightcap and got into bed, and waited for the child to knock at the door. But he waited a long time.

THE WOLF AT THE GRANDMOTHER'S COTTAGE.

By and by Little Red Riding-Hood reached her grandmother's house, and tapped at the door.

RED RIDING HOOD AT HER GRANDMOTHER'S DOOR.

"Come in," said the wolf, in a squeaking voice. "Pull the string, and the latch will come up."

Red Riding-Hood thought grandmother must have a cold, she spoke so hoarsely; but she went in at once, and there lay her granny, as she thought, in bed.

"If you please, grandmamma, mother sends you some butter and eggs," she said.

"Come here, dear," said the wicked wolf, "and let me kiss you," and Red Riding-Hood obeyed.

THE WOLF AND THE CHILD.

But when Red Riding-Hood saw the wolf she felt frightened. She had nearly forgotten grandmother, but she did not think she had been so ugly.

"Grandmamma," she said, "what a great nose you have."

"All the better to smell with, my dear," said the wolf.

"And, grandmamma, what large ears you have."

"All the better to hear with, my dear."

"Ah! grandmamma, and what large eyes you have."

"All the better to see with, my dear," said the wolf, showing his teeth, for he longed to eat the child up.

"Oh, grandmamma, and what great teeth you have!" said Red Riding-Hood.

LITTLE RED RIDING HOOD DISCOVERS THE WOLF.

"All the better to eat you up with," growled the wolf, and, jumping out of bed, he rushed at Red Riding-Hood and would have eaten her up, but just at that minute the door flew open and a great dog tore him down. The wolf and the dog were still fighting when Hugh, the woodman, came in and killed the wicked wolf with his axe.

DEATH OF THE WOLF.

DEATH OF THE WOLF.

Little Red Riding-Hood threw her arms round the woodman Hugh's neck and kissed him, and thanked him again and again.

"Oh, you good, kind Hugh," she said, "how did you know the wolf was here, in time to save me?"

"Well," said Hugh, "when you were gone by, I remembered that a wolf had been seen about the wood lately, and I thought I would just come after you and see if you were safe. When we came near grandmother's house Trim sniffed and ran to the door and whined, and then he pushed it open—you had not shut it close—and rushed in, and I followed him, and between us we have killed the wolf."

Then Hugh took the child home, and her mother and father could not thank him enough for saving Little Red Riding-Hood.

PUSS IN BOOTS.

Once upon a time there was a miller who had three sons. When he died he left his mill to the eldest son, his ass to the second son, and his cat to the youngest, who had always been his favourite.

The two eldest sons resolved to live together; but they would not let their brother live with them, because he had only a cat. So the poor lad was very sorrowful, and wondered what he should do to get his bread. While he was sitting thinking about it, Puss jumped up on the table, and touched him with her paw.

PUSS CONSOLING THE MILLER'S SON.

"My dear master," she said, "do not fret. I will get your living for you. Only you must buy me a pair of boots and give me a bag."

PUSS CATCHING THE RABBITS.

The miller's son had very little money, but he thought it such a wonderful thing to hear a cat talk that he could not refuse her request. So he took Puss to the shoemaker's, and got him to make her a very smart pair of boots, and then he gave her a nice large bag.

THE RABBIT WARREN.

Now, not far from the mill there was a rabbit warren, and Puss resolved to catch some rabbits for dinner. So she put some lettuce leaves and fine parsley into her bag, went into the warren, and held the bag very quietly open, hiding herself behind it. And little greedy rabbits, who knew no better, ran into it, to have a feast. Directly they were safe in, Puss pulled the string of the bag, and carried them off to her master. The miller's son killed them, and cooked one for dinner; but Puss took away the other, which was a very fine one, and hung it up for their next day's meal.

But although their larder was thus provided, early the next day Puss took her bag and went again into the warren, and in the same manner caught two more fine young rabbits. But instead of carrying them home she walked to the king's palace and knocked at the door.

PUSS AT THE PALACE.

The king's porter asked who was there. "I have brought a present to the king," said Puss. "Please let me see his majesty."

The porter let her in, and when Puss came into the king's presence she made a low bow, and, taking a fine rabbit out of her bag, said, "My Lord Marquis of Carrabas sends this rabbit to your majesty with his respects."

PUSS MAKES A PRESENT TO THE KING.

"I am much obliged to the marquis," said the king, and he ordered his head cook to dress the rabbit for dinner.

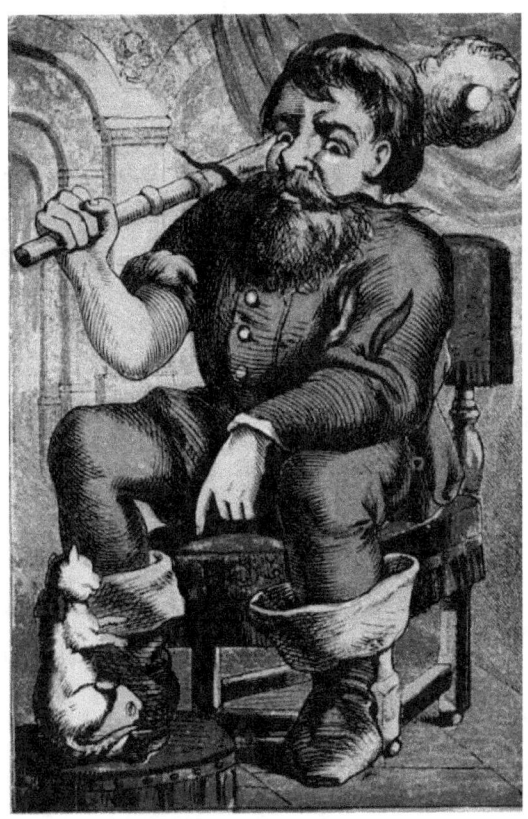

PUSS CALLS ON THE OGRE.

By the king's side sat his daughter, a very beautiful lady. She ordered one of the attendants to give Puss a good cup of cream, which she liked very much; and she went home and told her master all she had done. The miller's son laughed; but every morning Puss caught a rabbit, and carried it to the palace with the same message.

THE OGRE.

Now, in that country there lived a cruel ogre, who used to eat children, so everybody was afraid of him; but nobody could kill him, he was such a giant. One day Puss went to call on him. He received her civilly, for he did not care to eat cats, so Puss sat down, and began to talk:—"I hear," she said, "great Ogre, that you are so clever, that you can turn yourself into any creature you please."

"Yes, so I can," said the ogre.

"Dear me," said Puss, "how much I should like to see your ogreship do it."

Then the ogre, who liked to show how clever he was, turned himself into a lion, and roared so loudly that Puss was quite frightened, and jumped out of the way. Then he changed back into an ogre again. Puss praised him a great deal, and then said, "Can your ogreship become a small animal as well as a large one?"

"Oh, yes," said the vain ogre; and he changed himself into a little mouse. Directly Puss saw him in this form she jumped at him and killed him on the spot.

THE MARQUIS OF CARRABAS.

Then Puss ran home and bade her master go and bathe in the river, and he should see what she would do for him. The miller's son obeyed; and while he was in the water, Puss took away all his clothes, and hid them under a large stone. Now, the king's carriage came in sight soon after, just as Puss had expected, for he always drove in that direction, and directly she saw it, she began to cry very loudly, "Help, help, for my Lord the Marquis of Carrabas." The king put his head out, and asked what was the matter.

PUSS ASKS HELP FOR HIS MASTER.

"Oh, your majesty," said Puss, "my master the marquis was bathing, and some one has taken away his clothes. He will catch the cramp and be drowned."

PUSS THREATENS THE REAPERS.

Then the king ordered one of his attendants to ride back to the palace and get a suit of his own clothes for the marquis, "who had so often sent him gifts," he said. And when they were brought, Puss took them to her master, and helped him to dress in them.

PUSS FRIGHTENS THE REAPERS.

The miller's son looked quite like a gentleman in the king's clothes, and when he went to thank his majesty for them, the king asked him to get into the coach and he would drive him home. Then Puss told the coachman where to go, and ran on before and came to some reapers. "Reapers," said she, "if the king asks you whose field this is, say it belongs to the Marquis of Carrabas; if you don't say so, you shall be chopped up as small as mincemeat."

The reapers were so frightened that they promised to obey her. And she ran on and told all the other labourers on the road to say the same. So when the king asked, "To whom do these fine fields belong?" the reapers answered, "To the Marquis of Carrabas." The herdsmen said the same of the cattle, and the king, turning to the miller's son, said, "My lord, you have a fine property." But all had belonged really to the ogre, for it was to his castle the cunning cat had told the coachman to drive.

THE CASTLE.

At last the coach stopped at the Ogre's castle, and Puss came out, and bowing very low, said, "Your majesty and the princess are welcome to the castle of my Lord Marquis of Carrabas."

THE KING AND PRINCESS VISIT THE MARQUIS.

The king was delighted, for it was indeed a very nice castle, full of riches. They sat down to a great feast, which Puss ordered to be served, and the king was so pleased with the miller's son and thought him such a good match for the princess, that he invited him to court, and in a little while gave him his daughter for his wife, and made him a prince.

MARRIAGE OF THE MARQUIS AND PRINCESS.

You may be quite sure that the miller's son was very grateful to Puss for his good fortune, and she never had to catch mice for her dinner any more, for dainty meat and the best cream were every day given to Puss in Boots.

OLD MOTHER HUBBARD.

Old Mother Hubbard
Went to the cupboard
To get her poor Dog a bone;
But when she came there
The cupboard was bare,
And so the poor Dog had none.

OLD MOTHER HUBBARD AND HER DOG.

She went to the baker's
To buy him some bread,
But when she came back
The poor Dog looked dead.

THE DOG LOOKING DEAD.

She went to the hatter's
To buy him a hat,
But when she came back
He was feeding the cat.

She went to the barber's
To buy him a wig,
But when she came back
He was dancing a jig.

She went to the joiner's
To buy him a coffin,
But when she came back
The poor Dog was laughing.

She took a clean dish
To get him some tripe,
But when she came back
He was smoking a pipe.

THE DOG SMOKING A PIPE.

THE DOG STANDING ON HIS HEAD.

She went to the ale-house
To get him some beer,
But when she came back
The Dog sat in a chair.

She went to the tavern
For white wine and red,
But when she came back
The Dog stood on his head.

She went to the fruiterer's
To buy him some fruit,
But when she came back
He was playing the flute.

She went to the tailor's,
To buy him a coat,
But when she came back
He was riding a goat.

THE DOG PLAYING THE FLUTE.

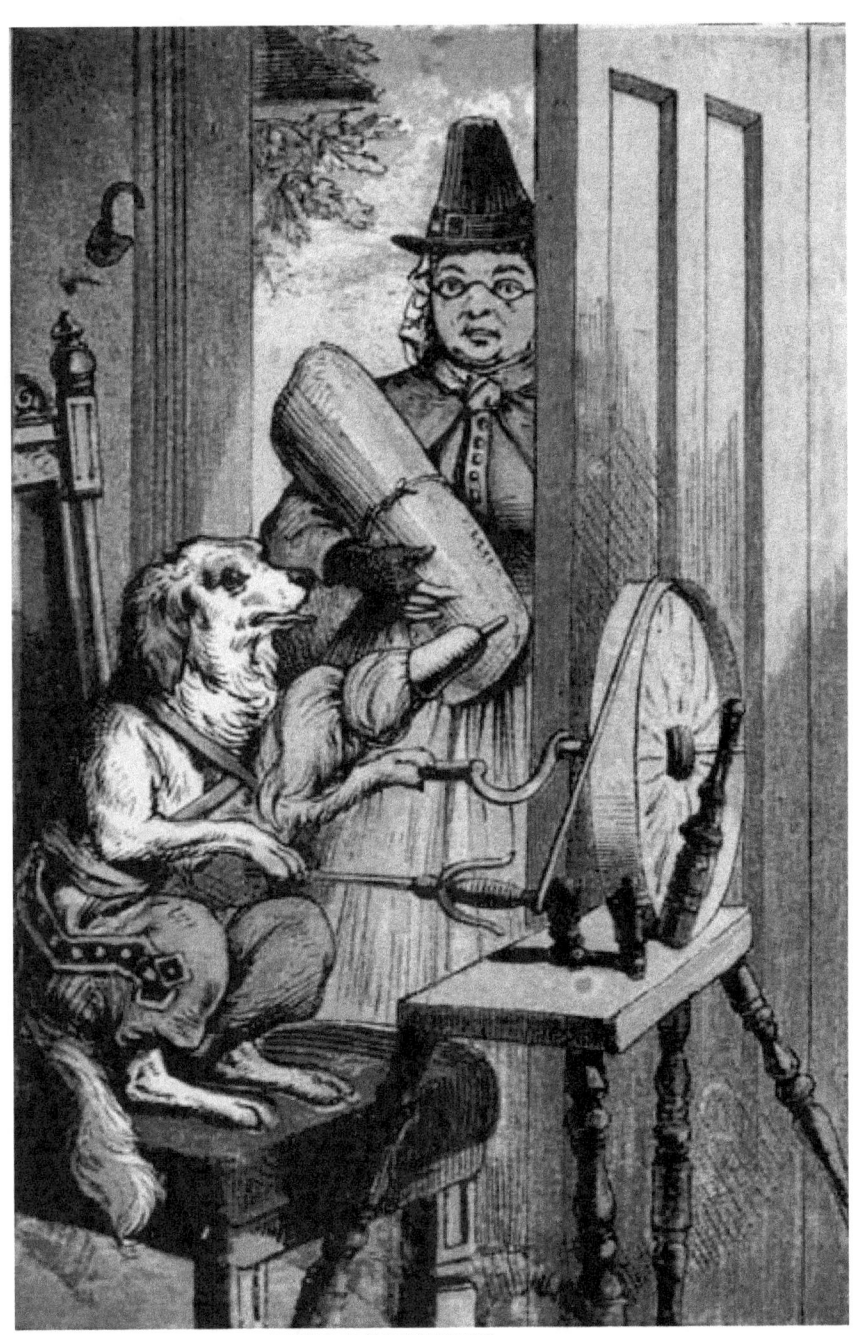

THE DOG SPINNING.

She went to the sempstress
To buy him some linen,
But when she came back
The Dog was a-spinning.

She went to the hosier's
To buy him some hose,
But when she came back
He was dressed in his clothes.

She went to the cobbler's
To buy him some shoes,
But when she came back
He was reading the news.

The Dame made a curtsey,
The Dog made a bow;
The Dame said, "Your servant;"
The Dog said, "Bow-wow!"

THE DOG READING THE NEWS.

THE DOG MADE A BOW.

This wonderful Dog
Was Dame Hubbard's delight;
He could sing, he could dance,
He could read, he could write.

So she gave him rich dainties
Whenever he fed,
And erected a monument
When he was dead.

COCK ROBIN.

Who killed Cock Robin?
I, said the Sparrow,
With my bow and arrow.
I killed Cock Robin.

THE SPARROW, COCK ROBIN, AND THE FISH.

THE LINNET, THE DOVE, AND COCK ROBIN.

Who saw him die?
I, said the Fly,
With my little eye.
I saw him die.

Who caught his blood?
I, said the Fish,
With my little dish.
I caught his blood.

Who'll carry him to the grave?
I, said the Kite,
If it's not in the night.
I'll carry him to the grave.

Who'll carry the link?
I, said the Linnet,
I'll fetch it in a minute.
I'll carry the link.

THE KITE AND COCK ROBIN.

THE OWL, THE BEETLE, AND COCK ROBIN.

Who'll make his shroud?
I, said the Beetle,
With my thread and needle.
I'll make his shroud.

Who'll dig his grave?
I, said the Owl,
With my spade and shovel.
I'll dig his grave.

Who'll toll the bell?
I, said the Bull,
Because I can pull.
I'll pull the bell.

THE BULL TOLLING THE BELL

THE ROOK AND THE LARK

Who'll be the Parson?
I, said the Rook,
With my little book.
I'll be the Parson.

Who'll be the Clerk?
I, said the Lark,
If it's not in the dark.
I'll be the Clerk.

Who'll be chief mourner?
I, said the Dove,
For I mourn for my love.
I'll be chief mourner.

Who'll sing a psalm?
I, said the Thrush,
As she sat in a bush.
I'll sing a psalm.

THE THRUSH.

SIGHING AND SOBBING FOR POOR COCK ROBIN.

All the birds of the air
Fell a-sighing and sobbing
When they heard the bell toll
For poor Cock Robin.

JACK & THE BEAN-STALK.

Once upon a time there was a poor widow who lived in a little cottage with her only son Jack.

JACK SELLS A COW FOR SOME BEANS.

Jack was a giddy, thoughtless boy, but very kind-hearted and affectionate. There had been a hard winter, and after it the poor woman had suffered from fever and ague. Jack did no work as yet, and by degrees they grew dreadfully poor. The widow saw that there was no means of keeping Jack and herself from starvation but by selling her cow; so one morning she said to her son, "I am too weak to go myself, Jack, so you must take the cow to market for me, and sell her." Jack liked going to market to sell the cow very much; but as he was on the way, he met a butcher who had some beautiful beans in his hand. Jack stopped to look at them, and the butcher told the boy that they were of great value, and persuaded him to sell the cow for them! And Jack was so silly as to consent to this foolish bargain.

THE BEAN-STALK GROWS OUT OF SIGHT IN A NIGHT.

When he brought them home to his mother instead of the money she expected for her nice cow, she was very vexed and shed many tears, scolding Jack for his folly. He was very sorry; but, he said, he might as well make the best of his bargain, so he put the seed-beans into the ground close by the side of the steep hill under shelter of which their cottage was built, and went to bed. The next morning when he got up, he found that the beans had grown, till the bean stalks reached right over the top of the hill, and were lost to his sight. Greatly surprised, he called his mother, and they both gazed in silent wonder at the bean-stalk, which was not only of great height, but was thick enough to bear Jack's weight.

"I wonder where it goes?" said Jack to his mother; "I think I will climb up and see."

His mother wished him not to venture up this strange ladder, but Jack coaxed her to give her consent to the attempt, for he was certain there must be something wonderful in the bean-stalk.

Jack instantly began to climb, and went up and up on the ladder-like bean till every thing he had left behind him, the cottage, the village, and even the tall church tower, looked quite little, and still he did not see the top of the bean stalk.

Jack felt a little tired, and thought for a moment that he would go back again; but he was a very persevering boy, and he knew that the way to succeed in anything is not to give up. So after resting for a moment he went on, and at last reached the top of the bean, and found himself in a beautiful country, finely wooded; and not far from the place where he had got off the bean-stalk stood a fine and strong castle.

Jack wondered very much that he had never heard of or seen this castle before; but when he reflected on the subject, he saw that it was as much separated from the village by the perpendicular rock on which it stood as if it were in another land.

While Jack was standing looking at the castle, a very strange-looking woman came out of the wood and advanced towards him.

JACK CLIMBS THE BEAN-STALK.

Jack took off his hat to the old lady, and she said, pointing to the castle, "Boy, that castle belongs to you. A wicked giant killed your father, and took it from your mother; try and win it back from the monster who now has it." As she ceased speaking she suddenly disappeared, and of course Jack knew she was a fairy.

JACK ASKS ABOUT THE CASTLE.

He was much surprised; however, he walked up to the castle door and knocked, and an old giantess came out. She did not wait till he spoke, but pulled him in at once, for she thought he would make a nice supper for her when her husband was asleep. Just at that moment, however, she heard the giant's step approaching, so she put Jack into a press, and told him to hide there, or the giant would eat him. As soon as the Ogre came in, he cried in a terrible voice

"Fee, fa, fie, fo, fum,
I smell the breath of an Englishman."

"Oh!" said his wife, "there is nobody here. You only smell a crow that is flying over the chimney." Then the giant sat down to dinner, which was quite ready, and when he had eaten a whole sheep, he said, "Bring me my hen."

The giantess brought a hen, and put it on the table before him, and then she went away. "Lay," said the giant to the hen, and she laid a golden egg. Jack could see quite plainly through a little hole which he had bored in the door. Three times the giant said "Lay," and each time the hen laid a solid gold egg. Then the Ogre, being drowsy, shut his eyes, and soon snored very loudly. Directly Jack found that the giant was asleep, he stole out of the press, caught up the hen, ran out of the room, opened the door of the castle, which the giant had left ajar, and descended the bean-stalk as fast as he could go. His mother was glad to see him again, and much surprised at seeing the hen, which laid them three gold eggs every day. Jack's mother took them to the next town and sold them, and soon grew quite rich. Some time afterwards Jack made another journey up the bean-stalk to the giant's castle; but first he dyed his hair and disguised himself. The old woman did not know him again, and dragged him in as she had done before to eat him by-and-by; but once more she heard her husband coming and hid him in the press, not thinking that it was the same boy who had stolen the hen. She put him into the same press, and bade him stay quite still there, or the giant would eat him.

THE HEN THAT LAYS GOLDEN EGGS.

Then the giant came in, saying:

"Fee, fa, fie, fo, fum,
I smell the breath of an Englishman."

"Oh!" said his wife, "it is only the cowherd, who has just been here.
We cannot spare him for your dinner."

JACK TAKES THE GIANT'S MONEY-BAGS.

Then the giant sat down, and when he had eaten half an ox, he told
his wife to bring his money-bags to him. She instantly went and

fetched two large bags full of gold; and then left him to go about her usual house-work.

The Ogre counted out the gold twice over, and then put it into the bags and tied them up. In a few minutes Jack heard him snore. He directly crept out of the press, seized the bags, and hurrying out of the castle, carried them home quite safely. Jack's mother was glad to see him safe at home again, and for a long time she would not let him go up the bean-stalk; but Jack knew he had not yet obeyed the fairy's command to win back the castle, so after a time he set off once more on this adventure, and tapped again at the castle door.

The giantess, who was very stupid, did not know him again, but she stopped a minute before she took him in. She feared another robbery; but Jack's fresh cheeks looked so tempting that she could not resist him, and so she bade him come in.

But at that moment she heard her husband's step approaching.

Afraid of losing her supper, the Ogress at once shut Jack in the press; and she had hardly hidden him when the giant came in, saying as usual,

"Fee, fa, fie, fo, fum,
"I smell the blood of an Englishman."

"Oh no!" said his wife, "it is only the shepherd, who has been up with a sheep for your dinner."

The giant sat down, and when he had eaten a whole sheep he said, "I should like some music; bring me my harp."

The Ogress went and brought a golden harp to him, set it on the table, and went away. Then the Ogre said, "Play," to the harp, and it played so delightfully that Jack was charmed.

JACK TAKES THE TALKING HARP.

By-and-by, however, the giant snored so loud that he could not hear the music; and Jack quickly stole out, and seizing the harp, ran away with it. But the harp was a fairy belonging to the giant, and as Jack ran, it cried out, "Master! Master!" The giant woke up slowly and rushed after Jack, but the boy was very nimble and outran him. You may imagine how fast Jack went down the bean-stalk this time, hearing all the while the tramp of the giant's feet behind him.

THE GIANT BREAKS HIS NECK.

Just as he reached the bottom he saw the Ogre looking down on him.

The next moment his great feet were on the bean-stalk.

"Mother, mother! bring me the axe," cried Jack.

His mother hastened with it, and just as the giant was half way down the bean-stalk, Jack succeeded in chopping it in halves; the lower half fell; the upper half swung away, and the giant, losing his hold, fell heavily to the ground on his head and broke his neck.

The same moment the fairy again stood beside Jack, and touching the broken bean-stalk was turned into a flight of broad, easy steps.

"Go up," she said, "and take possession of your own home, so long kept from you. The Ogress is dead, and there is no more danger. You have been brave and good. May you be happy."

Jack thanked the fairy very warmly for her aid, and she again departed to Fairyland, after explaining to Jack that she had been the butcher who sold him the beans.

TOM THUMB.

In the days of good king Arthur there lived a countryman and his wife who, though they had plenty to eat and to drink, and a very comfortable cottage to live in, were not at all happy.

They had no children, and they both wished very much for a baby. The wife was often in tears when her husband was out at work and she was all alone, because she had not an infant to take care of and nurse. One day, as she sat weeping by herself, more than usually sad, she said aloud, "If I only had a dear little baby, I should not care what it was like. I should be thankful for one if it were *no bigger than my husband's thumb.*"

Now it happened that the Queen of the Fairies was passing by, though the poor woman could not see her, and as she knew the farmer's wife was kind to the poor and likely to be a good mother, she thought she would grant her wish.

THE FARMER'S WIFE CRYING BECAUSE SHE HAS NO BABY.

So about an hour or two afterwards the woman was much surprised to see standing by the table a very beautiful lady, dressed splendidly, with a glittering star on her forehead and a wand in her right hand, with a gem of great brilliancy at the top of it. But what delighted the woman most of all was a tiny cradle, made of a walnut shell, lined with velvet, in which lay the prettiest baby ever seen, but it was only just as large as a man's thumb. "See," said the fairy, "your wish is granted. Here is a baby for you. Take care of it; it is your own." The woman did not know how to thank the fairy enough; she was so delighted, and the queen went away quite pleased at having given so much happiness.

THE FAIRY QUEEN BRINGING TOM THUMB TO HIS MOTHER.

Before the fairy went away, however, she gave the woman a little shirt of spider's web and a doublet of thistle-down for the baby.

When the farmer came home he was very much pleased. He invited all his friends to the christening, and the child was named "Tom," after him, and "Thumb," because he was no bigger than one.

The baby was very well, and merry, and grew, of course; but still it was very small.

However, at last Tom thought himself quite a great boy, and begged his mother to make him a little suit of clothes, and she made him one; but with a great deal of trouble, they were so small.

Tom was very often in mischief. He was so small that his mother used to put him on the table to play; and once she found him in the salt-box.

TOM FALLS INTO THE PUDDING.

One day she was making a plum-pudding, and Tom stood by the side of the basin, and peeped over the edge; but he could not see into it very well, and while his mother was gone for some more flour, he drew himself up on the edge of the basin. Alas! he fell in and disappeared in the wet pudding, which for poor Tom was a huge morass.

THE FALL OF THE PUDDING.

Tom would have cried out, but the pudding stuck his lips together, and his mother not missing him, stirred him up in the mixture, and put it and him into the pot. Tom no sooner felt the hot water than he danced about like mad; the woman was nearly frightened out of her wits to see the pudding come out of the pot and jump about, and she was glad to give it to a tinker who was passing that way. The tinker took the pudding and put it into a cloth, to carry it home to his family, who seldom tasted such a good dish.

But by-and-by, as he was climbing over a stile, he happened to squeeze it, and Tom, who had made quite an arch over his own head in the dry pudding by this time, cried out from the middle of it, "Hallo, Pickens!" which so terrified the tinker that he let the pudding drop in the field and scampered off as fast as he could. The pudding fell to pieces in the fall, and Tom, creeping out, went home to his mother, whom he found in great trouble, because she could not find him.

After this accident, Tom's mother never let him stay near her while she was cooking, but she was obliged to take him with her when she went out milking, for she dared not trust the little man in the house alone.

A few days after his escape from the pudding, Tom went, with his mother, into the fields to milk the cows, and for fear he should be blown away by the wind, she tied him to a thistle with a small piece of thread.

THE COW EATS TOM.

Very soon after, a cow eat up the thistle and swallowed Tom Thumb. His mother was in sad grief again; but Tom scratched and kicked in the cow's throat till she was glad to throw him out of her mouth again, and he was not at all hurt; but his mother became very anxious about her small son, who now gave her a great deal of trouble. Sometimes he fell into the milk-pail and was nearly drowned in the milk; once he was nearly killed by an angry chicken, and another time had a narrow escape from a cat.

THE EAGLE FLIES AWAY WITH TOM.

One day Tom went ploughing with his father, who gave him a whip made of a barley straw, to drive the oxen with; but an eagle, flying by, caught him up in his beak, and carried him to the top of a great giant's castle, and dropped him on the leads. The giant was walking on the battlements and thought at first that it was a foreign bird which lay at his feet, but soon seeing that it was a small man, he picked Tom up with his finger and thumb, and put the poor little creature into his great mouth, but the fairy dwarf scratched the roof of the giant's mouth, and bit his great tongue, and held on by his teeth till the ogre, in a passion, took him out again and threw him over into the sea, which ran beneath the castle walls. Here a very large fish swallowed him up directly.

Tom did not at all like swimming about in the fish, but by-and-by he felt it drawn upwards, and guessed at once that it was caught. And so it was; and being a very large fish, the fisherman thought it would make a good present for his beloved King Arthur. So he took it to the palace and begged the king to accept it.

King Arthur was pleased with the poor man's affection, and ordered the fish to be carried to the kitchen and cooked for his own dinner. The fisherman took it to the cook, who admired it very much, but said it was very heavy. Then he laid it on a table and began to cut it open. You may imagine how he jumped with fear and wonder when Tom Thumb slipped out of the fish!

The cook's cries brought the other servants, and soon everybody near ran to behold this wonder—the tiny man who came out of the fish.

Tom begged for some water to wash himself, and when he was clean, the courtiers thought him so pretty and such a marvel that they ran to tell the king about him.

TOM COMES OUT OF THE FISH.

Arthur was very much surprised; but he desired them to send the little man up after dinner to see him, and the Court tailor made haste at once to get ready a Court suit for Tom, which did not take him long to make; there were so few stitches in it!

KING ARTHUR RECEIVING TOM THUMB.

As soon as the king's great punch-bowl was set on the royal table, Tom Thumb was carried to see the monarch, who was delighted with the little man. Tom walked on the King's hand, and danced on the Queen's. He became a great favourite with Arthur, who made him a knight. Such is the wonderful history of Tom Thumb, who did much good when he grew older, and thus proved that however small people are, they may be of use in the world. He was good and kind to his parents, and to everybody; and the old ballad says,—

"Such were his deeds and noble acts
In Arthur's court there shone,
As like in all the world beside
Was hardly seen or known."

CINDERELLA.

Cinderella's mother died while she was a very little child, leaving her to the care of her father and her step-sisters, who were very much older than herself; for Cinderella's father had been twice married, and her mother was his second wife. Now, Cinderella's sisters did not love her, and were very unkind to her. As she grew older they made her work as a servant, and even sift the cinders; on which account they used to call her in mockery "Cinderella." It was not her real name, but she became afterwards so well known by it that her proper one has been forgotten.

She was a very sweet-tempered, good girl, however, and everybody (except her cruel sisters) loved her.

CINDERELLA AT HOME.

It happened, when Cinderella was about seventeen years old, that the King of that country gave a ball, to which all ladies of the land, and among the rest the young girl's sisters, were invited. And they made her dress them for the ball, but never thought of allowing her to go there.

CINDERELLA DRESSING HER SISTERS FOR THE BALL.

"I wish you would take me to the ball with you," said Cinderella, meekly.

"Take you, indeed!" answered the elder sister, with a sneer; "it is no place for a cinder-sifter: stay at home and do your work."

When they were gone, Cinderella, whose heart was very sad, sat down and cried bitterly; but as she sat sorrowful, thinking of the unkindness of her sisters, a voice called to her from the garden, and she went out to see who was there. It was her godmother, a good old Fairy.

"Do not cry, Cinderella," she said; "you also shall go to the ball, because you are a kind, good girl. Bring me a large pumpkin."

Cinderella obeyed, and the Fairy, touching it with her wand, turned it into a grand coach. Then she desired Cinderella to go to the trap, and bring her a rat. The girl obeyed, and a touch of the Fairy's wand turned him into a very smart coachman. Two mice were turned into footmen; four grasshoppers into white horses. Next, the Fairy touched Cinderella's rags, and they became rich satin robes, trimmed with point lace. Diamonds shone in her hair and on her neck and arms, and her kind godmother thought she had seldom seen so lovely a girl. Her old shoes became a charming pair of glass slippers, which shone like diamonds.

"Now go to the ball, my love," she said, "and enjoy yourself. But remember, you must leave the room before the clock strikes *eleven*. If you do not your dress will return to its original rags. I approve of pleasure, but not of dissipation, and I expect that you will show your gratitude by obeying me."

Cinderella kissed and thanked her godmother. Then she stepped into her coach and drove off, with her footmen behind, in great style. The Fairy, when she was gone, returned to Fairyland.

Cinderella was received at the King's palace with great respect. The Lord Chamberlain bowed low to her, thinking she must be a very great lady by her dress and carriage, and he showed her at once into the ball-room.

THE FAIRY GODMOTHER.

She was so beautiful that everybody looked at her, and wondered who she was; and the Prince asked her to dance with him, and afterwards would dance with no one else.

ARRIVAL AT THE PALACE.

But she made haste to leave a little before the hour fixed, and had time to undress before her sisters came home. They told her a beautiful Princess had been at the ball, with whom the Prince was delighted. They did not know it was Cinderella herself, and she was amused to hear them admire her grace and beauty, and say that they were sure she was a royal lady.

The Prince was quite vexed when supper-time came, and he could not find his beautiful partner, and no one had seen her leave the room. But in hopes of beholding her again, he persuaded the King to give another grand ball. As soon as her sisters were gone to it, Cinderella's godmother arrived.

"You were so good and obedient last time, that I shall let you go out again," said she to the young girl.

And once more the rat, mice, grasshoppers, and pumpkin (which had gone back to their original shapes after the first ball) were turned into the grand carriage and attendants, and Cinderella, in rose-coloured satin and rubies, went to the royal ball.

Directly the Prince saw her, he asked her to dance, and would have no other partner, and as he led her past her two unkind sisters, she saw them look at her dress with envious eyes, and knew that they wished they were as beautiful, and as well-dressed as she was.

But in the midst of her enjoyment, Cinderella remembered the Fairy's command, and at half-past ten glided out of the room, and drove home again. Her sisters found her waiting to undress them in her usual rags, and kept her up to tell her how beautiful the unknown Princess was, and how well she was dressed.

Again the Prince was vexed at the sudden disappearance of the beautiful stranger, and once more he persuaded the King to give a grand State ball.

"I wonder if Princess Beauty will be there!" said the sisters to Cinderella. "We must have new dresses, for she is so splendid. She makes every one look shabby."

CINDERELLA DANCES WITH THE PRINCE.

Cinderella smiled as she helped them to dress. She was sure the Fairy would let her go to the ball too. And she was right. Her godmother, pleased with her obedience, came in good time, and Cinderella, dressed in blue satin and pearls, went in the same style as before.

CINDERELLA RUNS HOME AND LOSES HER SLIPPER.

The Prince would scarcely let her out of his sight, and Cinderella, who was getting a little spoiled by all the flattery she heard, began to think more of herself and less of the Fairy; so the time stole on, till glancing up at the clock, she saw it wanted only five minutes to eleven.

At once she darted out of the room, and ran through the palace as fast as she could go, but as she reached the hall, she lost one of her precious glass slippers! She did not stop to pick it up, but rushed to the door. Alas! the clock had struck Eleven. She found no coach, only a pumpkin, and the rat and mice ran quickly away when they saw her; while all her fine dress turned to rags, and she had to run home alone in the darkness of the night.

The Prince was very much surprised when he missed Cinderella again, and leaving the ball, went in search of her. He asked all the attendants, but no one had seen her, and when enquiry was made of the porter, he said that no one had gone out of the palace except a poor ragged beggar-girl.

However, the Prince's search was rewarded by his finding the glass slipper, which he well knew belonged to the unknown Princess. He loved Cinderella so much that he now resolved to marry her; and as he felt sure that no one else could wear such a tiny shoe as hers was, he sent out a herald to proclaim that whichever lady in his kingdom could put on this glass slipper should be his wife.

All the great ladies who wished to be a Princess tried to put it on, but in vain. Cinderella's sisters tried, but could not get it on, and then Cinderella asked if she might try. They laughed at her; but the Prince, hearing of her wish, sent for her. She went with her sisters in her poor dress, but very clean, and at once put on the slipper. Then she drew the fellow of it from her pocket, and slipped it on her other foot.

The Prince, who had thought the moment he saw her that the poor girl was very much like the beautiful Princess, was delighted. He insisted on Cinderella telling him her story, which she did very modestly, and all listened with wonder.

CINDERELLA TRIES ON THE SLIPPER.

As her tale ended, the Fairy godmother suddenly entered the room, and placing her godchild's hand in the Prince's, said:

"Take this young girl for your wife, Prince; she is good and patient, and as she has known how to submit to injustice meekly, she will know how to reign justly."

CINDERELLA MARRIED TO THE PRINCE.

So Cinderella was married to the Prince in great state, and they lived together very happily. She forgave her sisters, and treated them always very kindly, and the Prince had great cause to be glad that he had found the glass slipper.

THE THREE BEARS.

Once upon a time three bears lived in a nice little house in a great forest.

There was the Father Bear, the Mother Bear, and the Baby Bear.

They had each a bed to sleep in, a chair to sit on, and a basin and spoon for eating milk or honey, which was their favourite food.

One morning the three bears resolved on taking a walk before breakfast; but before they went out, they poured their warm milk into their basins, that it might get cool by the time they came back.

THE BEARS AT BREAKFAST.

When the milk was poured out, the three bears set out for a walk.

THE BEARS OUT FOR A WALK.

Mr. and Mrs. Bear walked arm-in-arm, and Baby ran by their side.

"WHAT A FINE DAY IT IS!" growled Mr. Bear.

"What a fine day it is!" said Mrs. Bear.

"What a fine day!" squeaked little Bear.

And so it was.

The sun shone brightly though it was low in the sky, and its rays glittered on the fine webs on the grass. The leaves shivered in the soft breeze; the wood-pigeon cooed; the lark sang loud enough to make himself hoarse; the sparrows chirped; the bee buzzed, and a yellow butterfly perched on great Bear's nose.

"What a squeaky noise these creatures make!" said big Bear, as he brushed off the butterfly. "What a pity it is they have not *our* deep voices."

"Yes," said Mrs. Bear; "you have a much finer voice than the lark. I should like to hear him growl as you do."

"Oh, my dear, you are too kind; my growl is nothing to the lion's."

And thus conversing, the bears walked on.

Now there lived in the same forest a sweet little girl, who was called Golden Hair. She was the Woodman's daughter, and her hair looked just like sunbeams. She knew every tree in the greenwood, and every flower in it. She loved the birds, and liked to listen to their song; and everything in the wood loved Golden Hair. The trees bent down their lower branches to touch her glittering head as she passed; the birds sang sweeter as she glided by. The lark's song in the sky was—

"Come up, come up, Golden Hair; here is your happy home."

"Coo, I love you; coo, I love you!" cooed the wood-pigeon, as she passed.

"Twit, twit, pretty child," said the sparrow.

"Oh, you darling," sang the blackbird; and Golden Hair laughed with glee, for she liked to be loved.

LITTLE GOLDEN HAIR.

As to the butterflies, they flew after her, and rested on her hair, and tickled her cheeks; but she never tried to catch them.

GOLDEN HAIR PEEPING INTO THE BEARS' HOUSE.

She would not frighten or vex them for anything. She loved all the creatures, and that is why they loved her.

Love makes love.

Dear little Golden Hair, she went on singing merrily through the greenwood, saying sometimes to herself—

"I wish I could sing as well as the lark!"

By-and-by Little Golden Hair reached the Bears' house. She had never seen it before, and she wondered who lived there. A window was open, and Golden Hair peeped in.

"Dear me," thought the child, "whose house can it be! There is a table and three chairs, and three basins of hot milk, all steaming, and nobody to drink it. But I don't see any work or books, or anything else. I think I will go in and see who lives here."

So she tapped at the door, and cried, "Is any one at home?"

But there was no answer. Then Golden Hair stepped in very carefully, and looked about her.

She could not see any one, nor hear anybody snoring, so she walked into the Bears' parlour.

There was a fire, which made the room cheerful, and the hot milk looked very inviting; it quite seemed to say, "Come and have some breakfast;" and the early spring air had made Golden Hair rather cold, and very hungry; so she sat down by the fire in the little Bear's chair. It was too small for her, but she did not quite sit down at first. In a moment she got up again, and went round the table and tasted the milk in all the basins. Little Bear's was the nicest, because it had sugar in it, and Golden Hair thought it was good. So she took the basin and sat down again in Little Bear's chair, took his spoon, and ate up *all* his milk. Now this was very wrong. A tiny bear is only a tiny bear; still, he has a right to keep his own things. But Golden Hair did not know any better. Unluckily, Baby Bear's chair was, as we have said, too small for her; she broke the seat and fell through, basin and all.

GOLDEN HAIR EATS THE LITTLE BEAR'S BREAKFAST.

Then Golden Hair went upstairs, and there she saw three beds all in a row. Golden Hair lay down on Father Bear's bed first, but that was too long for her; then she lay down on Mother Bear's bed, and that was too wide for her; last of all she lay down on Baby Bear's bed, and there she fell asleep, for she was tired.

THE LITTLE BEAR GRIEVES FOR HIS BROKEN CHAIR.

By-and-by the bears came home. Baby Bear saw that his chair was broken and thrown down, and he cried in a very squeaky voice,

"Somebody has been here;" and Father Bear growled,

"SOMEBODY HAS BEEN HERE;"

And Mother Bear growled, more softly,

"Somebody has been here."

Then they went to the table and looked at their breakfasts, and Father Bear growled, "WHO HAS TOUCHED MY BASIN?"

And Mother Bear growled, "Who has touched my basin?"

And Tiny Bear squeaked, "Somebody has broken mine!"

And then Tiny Bear began to cry, for he was very fond of his own basin and his own chair; and, besides, he was very hungry after his long walk in the forest.

It really did seem a shame. Then the three bears thought they would go over their house, to see who had been in it, and to try if they could find the thief.

They went upstairs to their bedroom, which was over their other room, and as soon as they saw the tumbled beds Father Bear growled,

"WHO HAS BEEN LYING ON MY BED?"

And Mother Bear growled

"Who has been lying on my bed?"

And Tiny Bear squeaked out,

"Oh! here is a little girl in my bed; and it must be she who has eaten my breakfast and broken my chair."

THE BEARS FIND GOLDEN HAIR IN LITTLE BEAR'S BED.

Then Father Bear growled,

"LET US EAT HER UP;"

And Mother Bear growled, "Let us eat her up;"

And Tiny Bear squeaked,

"Let us eat her up."

GOLDEN HAIR ESCAPES FROM THE BEARS.

The noise they made woke Golden Hair, and you may imagine how
frightened she was when she saw the three bears. She started out
of bed, and jumped at once out of the window. The bears rushed
after her, and Father Bear caught her golden hair in his teeth, but
she left a lock behind, and still ran on. Then the three bears all

jumped out after her, but they fell one on the top of the other and rolled over and over, and while they were picking themselves up, little Golden Hair ran home, and they were not able to catch her.

But I do not think she had acted rightly (though she did not deserve to be eaten up); it was very wrong to break little Bear's chair and eat his milk, and I think Golden Hair will have to take great care to keep out of the reach of the Three Bears.

PUNCH AND JUDY.

Mr. Punch and his wife
Led a terrible life,
Very much like a dog and a cat;
Till, one summer morn
A baby was born,
A darling all dimples and fat.

PUNCH, JUDY, AND THE BABY.

Mrs. Judy was proud,
And the nurses allowed
That they never had seen such a child;
And the proud mother thought
When her baby she brought
To her husband, "It must make him mild."

PUNCH AND THE BABY.

Mr. Punch was quite pleased;
The poor baby he seized,
And danced up and down in great joy.

"Oh, my Judy," he cried,

"With a father's just pride,
I look on our beautiful boy."

But the baby soon cried;
Punch's temper was tried,
And in a great passion he flew;
He shook the poor child,
And, with rage growing wild,
The babe o'er the balcony threw.

Judy, greatly displeased,
A thick stick at once seized,
And began her stern husband to beat;
"O you monster," she cried,
As her weapon she plied,
"You deserve the same ending to meet."

PUNCH AND JUDY.

On his arms and his head
Her blows fell like lead;
She wonder'd such treatment he stood!
Beating and battering,
She made such a clattering,
It sounded like chopping up wood.

PUNCH KILLS JUDY.

Of his beating quite tired,
Punch's patience expired;
He snatched the stick out of her hands,
And gave Judy a blow
Which, alas, laid her low,
And above her a conqueror stands.

Then he danced and he sang,
And such nonsense began,
That we laughed, though we couldn't tell why;
For in such a sad case
It were much more our place
For Judy's misfortunes to cry.

PUNCH AND THE CONSTABLE.

But the constable see!—
"Are you come here for me?"
Cries Punch, as he dances about.
"Yes, yes; come to jail,
'Tis a terrible tale,"
Said the constable, "you must come out,

"And be tried for your life,
For thus killing your wife;
In prison, meantime, you'll abide."
"Oh no, I won't go,"
Cried Punch, and a blow
He gave the poor man in his side.

PUNCH, TOBY, AND THE CLOWN.

Now Punch had a pet
Whom we must not forget,
A dog known as Toby by name;
A clown from a show
One day came to know
If Punch would not sell him the same.

But Punch would not part
From his dog, for his heart
(Though a wooden one) to him was true.
He cried, "Give me a kiss,
Dear Toby, I wis
I never will sever from you."

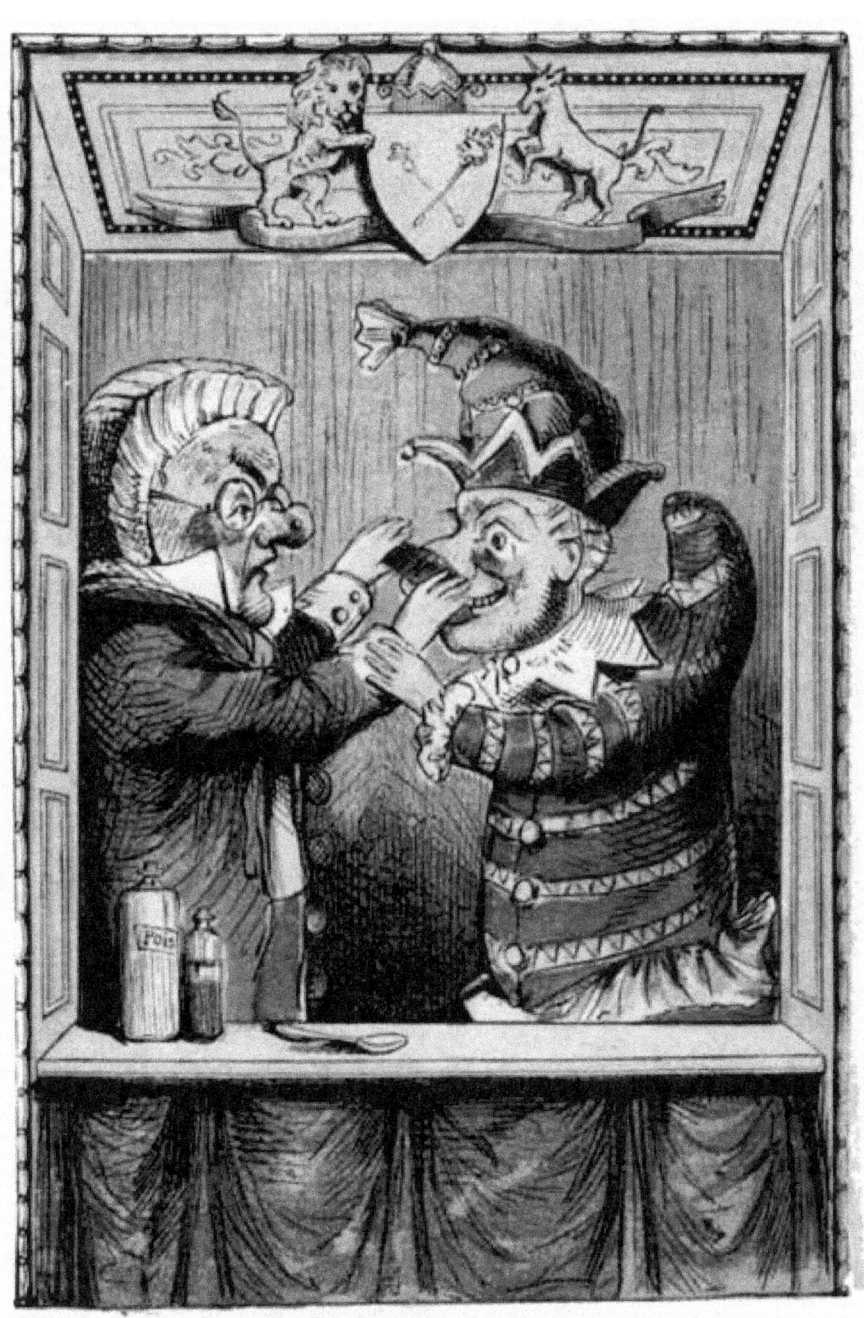

PUNCH AND THE DOCTOR.

But Jack Ketch comes at last;
Punch's frolics are past,
There is no one his cause to befriend;
His nonsense and fun
Are all, alas, done;
He has come to a very bad end!

If he were not of wood
It would not be good
To laugh at the harm he has done;
But 'twas only pretence,
And there was not much sense
In his crimes, or his grief, or his fun.

PUNCH AND JACK KETCH.

For a great many years,
Punch's laughter and tears,
Have amused both the child and the man;
So I think at the last,
For the sake of the past
We will keep him as long as we can.

THE PETS.

THE SHEEP.

The sheep is a very useful animal. Its wool, sheared off, makes us cloth and flannel, and all kinds of woollen goods; and its flesh, called mutton, is a chief part of our food. When sheep are little they are called lambs, and are very playful, pretty creatures.

SHEEP.

Sheep soon learn to know the voice of their shepherd, and will follow it. In Eastern countries the shepherd walks before his flock, and they are led by his voice. There are dogs called sheep-dogs, which take care of the flocks, and protect the sheep, and keep them together. In some countries these dogs have often to fight with wolves, which attack the sheep and carry them off whenever they can; but the dogs are quite able to keep the wolf away when they are trained to do so.

RABBITS.

On the Scottish hills the sheep-dog is often obliged to seek his charge in the snow-drifts, and to help get out a poor sheep or lamb which has got buried in it. Sheep love green meadows and pure water. You remember, I dare say, the beautiful Psalm, "The Lord is my shepherd, therefore I shall lack nothing."

RABBITS.

Are the favourite pets of boys. They are merry little creatures, and it is an amusing sight to watch them running over the green turf about their warren, when they are free. They have many enemies, however, such as dogs, foxes, and weasels. But, in spite of their enemies, rabbits live a merry life together.

There are a great many different kinds of tame rabbits; some are white, with pink eyes and long ears. Rabbits have many young ones. One pair will have fifty-six little rabbits in a year. So it is lucky many other creatures feed on them. If they were left to increase, they would soon eat up every stalk of corn and all the green herbs.

The native country of the rabbit is Spain. In the Orkney Islands, where there are great numbers of rabbits, the wild ones are of a grey colour, and in winter time almost white.

The fur of the rabbit is much used for making hats. They are good for food also.

THE COW.

Is a very valuable animal; indeed I do not know what we should do without her. She gives us milk and butter, cheese and cream; her skin is of great use, and her flesh is often eaten as beef. Cows grow fond of those who are kind to them.

COW AND CALF.

There are a great many different kinds of cows; some red, some black, some brindled, white or spotted. Herefordshire cows have white faces. The ancient Britons had great numbers of fine cows; and wild cattle were common in our country seven hundred years ago. In the neighbourhood of London, in Henry II.'s reign, there was a large forest which contained a great many wild bulls and cows.

THE DONKEY.

The cow is a good mother, very fond of her calf. The bull is a very bold, fierce animal. It has a great dislike to the colour red, and will run after and if it can toss any one wearing it. In Spain they have a cruel sport, called bull fights, between these brave animals and men on horseback.

The flesh of the cow and ox is called beef; that of the calf is veal.

THE DONKEY.

This patient and useful animal is supposed to have come at first from the East, where it still continues to be of a greater size and of a much better appearance. They were as valuable there in former ages as horses; great men and judges rode on asses. The ass is very fond of its foal, and can be attached to its master if kindly treated. Its milk is thought very good for consumptive people. It is very sure-footed, and strong, and able to carry heavy burdens.

The Donkey is a very useful animal to the poor. It can do a great deal of work on very coarse and cheap food. Thistles make a dainty dinner for the ass. It is patient and gentle, but occasionally very obstinate; a fault chiefly produced in the poor beast by ill-usuage.

Children should never be cruel to this poor animal, but treat it kindly, and it will not then be stubborn and slow, but will do its best to carry them.

THE COCK, THE HEN, AND THE CHICKENS.

Here is a fine farm-yard family! very useful friends of ours. The cock, who is a brave, spirited bird, wakes us up in the morning by crowing; the hen lays us eggs for breakfast, and when the wee chicks are big enough, they are very good food, as roast chicken. The cock teaches us watchfulness; the hen, motherly love.

THE COCK, THE HEN, AND THE CHICKENS.

There are many different kinds of fowls. The largest are the tall Cochin Chinas; the smallest the pert little Bantams. It is a great amusement for children to have a few fowls to feed, and take care of. Feeding them and finding their eggs is one of the country child's pleasures.

The hen sits on her eggs for three weeks; and when the chicks are hatched, she takes the greatest care of them, gathering them under her wings when danger is near or the weather is at all cold; and she is ready to fight a hawk or even a dog in defence of her little ones.

Fowls feed on barley or any kind of grain, and pick up worms, &c., in their run. Stinging-nettles are very good food for chickens.

THE HORSE.

This noblest of animals is believed to be a native of Arabia; but was in our islands before the Romans came here. The first money coined in Britain was stamped with the figure of a horse.

THE HORSE.

The horse has a wonderful memory. He never forgets a place to which he has once been taken. He loves his master if well treated; and in battles he displays the greatest courage and joy. He also understands sounds, and loves music. Indeed, the horse may be called the friend of man, and deserves all the kindness we can show him.

The Arabs bring up their horses with their children in their own tents; and the steed thus reared is very sensible and gentle. An Arab will not sell his favourite horse for any sum, however large: it is as dear to him as his children.

THE GOAT.

The goat is a very useful animal. Its flesh is very good, though English people seldom eat it. Its milk is very good also, and of use to people in consumption. The most beautiful gloves are made from its skin.

GOATS.

Goats abound on the Welsh mountains; it is, indeed, an animal that loves the great hills. The Welsh goats are white; they are very active, and walk on the brink of precipices, and take the most wonderful leaps. The scent of a goat is unpleasant, but it is thought to prevent infection amongst cattle.

Horses are very fond of goats. They are more common in France than with us. In that country one sees a goat with nearly every flock of sheep.

Goats' flesh is called "kid." Do you remember how Jacob deceived his father with the skin and meat of a kid of the goats?

PIGS.

NURSERY SONGS.

LITTLE MISS MUFFET.

Little Miss Muffet
She sat on a tuffet,
Eating of curds and whey.
There came a great spider,
Who sat down beside her,
And frightened Miss Muffet away.

PAT-A-CAKE, PAT-A-CAKE.

Pat-a-cake, Pat-a-cake, baker's man,
Make me a cake as fast as you can;
Pat it, and prick it, and mark it with T,
And send it home for Tommy and me.

Humpty Dumpty sat on a wall,
Humpty Dumpty had a great fall;
All the king's horses and all the king's men
Could not set Humpty Dumpty up again.

HUMPTY DUMPTY.

YOUNG LAMBS TO SELL!

Young lambs to sell!—young lambs to sell!
If I had as much money as I could tell,
I never would cry, Young lambs to sell!
Young lambs to sell!—young lambs to sell!
I never would cry, Young lambs to sell!

LITTLE ROBIN REDBREAST SAT UPON A TREE.

Little Robin Redbreast sat upon a tree,
Up went Pussy-cat, and down went he;
Down came Pussy-cat, and away Robin ran;
Says little Robin Redbreast, "Catch me if you can."
Little Robin Redbreast jumped upon a wall,
Pussy-cat jumped after him and almost got a fall;
Little Robin chirped and sang, and what did Pussy say?
Pussy-cat said "Mew," and Robin jumped away.

HANDY SPANDY, JACK-A-DANDY.

Handy Spandy Jack-a-Dandy
Loved plumcake and sugar candy;
He bought some at a grocer's shop,
And out he came, hop, hop, hop.

LITTLE BOY BLUE.

Little Boy Blue, come blow up your horn,
The sheep's in the meadow, the cow's in the corn.
Where's the little boy that looks after the sheep?
He is under the hay-cock fast asleep.

THIS LITTLE PIG WENT TO MARKET.

This little pig went to market;
This little pig stayed at home;
This pig had a piece of bread-and-butter;
This little pig had none;
This little pig said, "Wee, wee, wee!
I can't find my way home."

NURSERY RHYMES.

LITTLE JACK HORNER.

Little Jack Horner sat in a corner,
Eating his Christmas Pie;
He put in his thumb, and pulled out a plum,
And said, "What a good boy am I!"

TO MARKET, TO MARKET.

To market, to market, to buy a fat pig;
Home again, home again, jiggetty-jig.
To market, to market, to buy a fat hog;
Home again, home again, jiggetty-jog.

Taffy was a Welshman,
Taffy was a thief;
Taffy came to my house
And stole a piece of beef.
I went to Taffy's house,
Taffy was from home;
Taffy came to my house
And stole a marrow bone.

TAFFY WAS A WELSHMAN.

BAA, BAA, BLACK SHEEP.

Baa, baa, black sheep,
Have you any wool?
Yes, marry, have I,
Three bags full:
One for my master,
One for my dame;
But none for the little girl
That cries in the lane.

PRETTY MAID, PRETTY MAID.

Pretty maid, pretty maid, where have you been?
Gathering a posie to give to the Queen.

MARY, MARY, QUITE CONTRARY.

Mary, Mary, quite contrary,
How does your garden grow?
Silver bells and cockle-shells,
And columbines all of a row.

LITTLE BO-PEEP.

Little Bo-Peep has lost his sheep,
And cannot tell where to find them
Leave them alone, and they'll come home,
And bring their tails behind them.

Little Bo-Peep fell fast asleep,
And dreamt he heard them bleating
When he awoke, he found it a joke,
For still they all were fleeting.

Then up he took his little crook,
Determined for to find them;
He found them indeed, but it made his heart bleed,
For they'd left their tails behind them.

HOT CROSS BUNS.

Hot Cross Buns!
Hot Cross Buns!
One a penny, two a penny, Hot Cross Buns.
Hot Cross Buns!
Hot Cross Buns!
If you have no daughters, give them to your sons.

THE CAT AND FIDDLE.

Hey diddle diddle,
The cat and the fiddle,
The cow jumped over the moon,
The little dog laughed
To see the sport,
While the dish ran after the spoon.

THE QUEEN OF HEARTS.

The Queen of Hearts,
She made some tarts
Upon a summer day;
The Knave of Hearts,
He stole those tarts,
And took them quite away.

The King of Hearts,
He missed those tarts,
And beat the knave full sore;
The Knave of Hearts
Brought back those tarts,
And vowed he'd steal no more.

I HAD A LITTLE HUSBAND.

I had a little husband,
No bigger than my thumb;
I put him in a pint-pot,
And there I bid him drum.

I bought a little horse,
That galloped up and down;
I bridled him and saddled him,
And sent him out of town.

I gave him some garters,
To garter up his hose,
And a little handkerchief
To wipe his pretty nose.

GOOSEY, GOOSEY, GANDER.

Goosey, Goosey Gander,
Where shall I wander?
Up stairs, down stairs,
In my lady's chamber.

There I met an old man
That would not say his prayers;
I took him by the left leg,
And threw him down stairs.

LITTLE POLLY FLINDERS.

Little Polly Flinders,
Sat among the cinders,
Warming her pretty little toes;
Her mother came and caught her,
And scolded her little daughter,
For spoiling her nice new clothes.

DING DONG BELL.

Ding Dong Bell,
Pussy's in the well.
Who put her in?
Little Tommy Lin.
Who pulled her out?
Little Tommy Trout.
What a naughty boy was that,
To drown poor little Pussy cat,
Who never did him any harm,
But killed the mice in his father's barn.

"MULTIPLICATION IS VEXATION."

Multiplication is vexation;
Division is as bad;
The Rule of Three doth puzzle me,
And Practice drives me mad.

THE DAPPLE-GREY PONY.

I had a little pony,
His name was Dapple Grey,
I lent him to a lady,
To ride a mile away.

She whipped him, she slashed him,
She rode him through the mire;
I would not lend my pony now,
For all the lady's hire.

OLD WOMAN, OLD WOMAN, SAYS I.

Old woman, old woman, old woman say I,
O whither, O whither, O whither so high?
To sweep the cobwebs off the sky.
Shall I go with you? Ay, by-and-by.

DAME TROT AND HER CAT.

Dame Trot and her cat
Led a peaceable life
When they were not troubled
With other folks' strife.

When Dame had her dinner
Puss near her would wait,
And was sure to receive
A nice piece from her plate.

SIMPLE SIMON.

Simple Simon met a pieman
Going to the fair;
Says Simple Simon to the pieman,
"Let me taste your ware."

Says the pieman to Simple Simon,
"Show me first your penny."
Says Simple Simon to the pieman,
"Indeed, I have not any."

Simple Simon went a-fishing
For to catch a whale;
All the water he had got
Was in his mother's pail.

MARY HAD A PRETTY BIRD.

Mary had a pretty bird,
With feathers bright and yellow,
Slender legs—upon my word,
He was a pretty fellow.

The sweetest notes he always sang,
Which much delighted Mary;
And near the cage she'd ever sit,
To hear her own Canary.

IS JOHN SMITH WITHIN?

Is John Smith within?
Yes, that he is.
Can he set a shoe?
Ay, marry, two;
Here a nail and there a nail,
Tick, tack, too.

GUY FAWKES.

Please to remember
The fifth of November,
Gunpowder treason and plot.
I know no reason
Why gunpowder treason
Should ever be forgot.

JACK AND JILL.

Jack and Jill went up the hill
To fetch a pail of water.
Jack fell down and broke his crown,
And Jill came tumbling after.

LITTLE FRED.

When little Fred went to bed,
He always said his prayers.
He kissed mamma and then papa,
And straightway went upstairs.

LITTLE TOM TUCKER.

Little Tommy Tucker,
Sings for his supper.
What shall he eat?
White bread and butter.
How shall he cut it
Without e'er a knife?
How will he be married
Without e'er a wife.

WHERE ARE YOU GOING, MY PRETTY MAID?

Where are you going, my pretty maid?
I'm going a milking, sir, she said.
May I go with you, my pretty maid?
You're kindly welcome, sir, she said.
What is your fortune, my pretty maid?
My face is my fortune, sir, she said.
Then I won't marry you, my pretty maid.
Nobody asked you, sir, she said.

RIDE A COCK-HORSE.

Ride a cock-horse to Banbury Cross,
To see an old lady upon a white horse;
Rings on her fingers and bells on her toes,
And so she makes music wherever she goes.

SING A SONG OF SIXPENCE.

Sing a song of sixpence,
A bag full of rye;
Four-and-twenty blackbirds
Baked in a pie.

When the pie was opened
The birds began to sing.
Was not that a dainty dish
To set before the king?

The king was in his countinghouse,
Counting out his money;
The queen was in the parlour,
Eating bread and honey.

The maid was in the garden,
Hanging out the clothes;
'Long came a blackbird
And snapt off her nose.

TOM, TOM, THE PIPER'S SON.

Tom, Tom, the piper's son,
Stole a pig and away he run!
The pig was eat, and Tom was beat,
And Tom went roaring down the street.

OLD KING COLE.

Old King Cole
Was a merry old soul,
And a merry old soul was he!
He called for his pipe,
And he called for his bowl,
And he called for his fiddlers three.

Every fiddler he had a fiddle,
And a very fine fiddle had he!
Twee tweedle dee, tweedle dee went the fiddlers.
Oh, there's none so rare
As can compare
With King Cole and his fiddlers three!

FOUR-AND-TWENTY TAILORS WENT TO KILL A SNAIL.

Four-and-twenty tailors went to kill a snail;
The best man among them durst not touch her tail.
She put out her horns like a little Kyloe cow.
Run, tailors, run, or she'll kill you all e'en now.

HUSH-A-BY BABY.

Hush-a-by, baby, thy cradle is green;
Father's a nobleman; mother's a queen;
Betty's a lady, and wears a gold ring,
And Johnny's a drummer and drums for the king.

End of the book.

www.ingramcontent.com/pod-product-compliance
Lightning Source LLC
Chambersburg PA
CBHW070006300526
45794CB00001B/203